# WOMEN IN SCIENCE

D1414464

# CHIEN-SHIUNG WU

## NUCLEAR PHYSICIST

by Nel Yomtov

Content Consultant
Suzanne Keilson, PhD
Assistant Professor, Department of Engineering
Loyola University Maryland

**Essential Library**

An Imprint of Abdo Publishing | abdopublishing.com

ABDOPUBLISHING.COM

Published by Abdo Publishing, a division of ABDO, PO Box 398166, Minneapolis, Minnesota 55439. Copyright © 2018 by Abdo Consulting Group, Inc. International copyrights reserved in all countries. No part of this book may be reproduced in any form without written permission from the publisher. Essential Library™ is a trademark and logo of Abdo Publishing.

Printed in the United States of America, North Mankato, Minnesota
042017
092017

**THIS BOOK CONTAINS RECYCLED MATERIALS**

Cover Photo: Gjon Mili/The LIFE Picture Collection/Getty Images
Interior Photos: PF-(bygone1)/Alamy, 4, 67; Photo Researchers Inc/Alamy, 8, 22, 97; SPL/Science Source, 10; Pictures From History/Newscom, 15; Robert W. Kelley/The LIFE Picture Collection/Getty Images, 18; Bettmann/Getty Images, 21, 43, 83; Ernest K. Bennett/AP Images, 25; Underwood Archives/Archive Photos/Getty Images, 29; Emilio Segre Visual Archives/American Institute of Physics/Science Source, 31, 50, 53, 76, 84; Everett Collection/Newscom, 32, 45; Peter Hermes Furian/iStockphoto, 35, 46; AIP Emilio Segre Visual Archives/Segre Collection/American Institute of Physics, 36; Shutterstock Images, 44; CTBTO/Flickr, 48; Science Source, 55, 62, 64–65, 81; John Lent/AP Images, 57; Francois Guillot/AFP/Getty Images, 61; James Burke/The LIFE Picture Collection/Getty Images, 69; Wen Ming Ming/Shutterstock Images, 87; iStockphoto, 90; Courtesy Gerald R. Ford Presidential Library, 93

Editor: Sue Bradley
Series Designer: Nikki Farinella

### PUBLISHER'S CATALOGING-IN-PUBLICATION DATA

Names: Yomtov, Nel, author.
Title: Chien-Shiung Wu: nuclear physicist / by Nel Yomtov.
Other titles: Nuclear physicist
Description: Minneapolis, MN : Abdo Publishing, 2018. | Series: Women in science | Includes bibliographical references and index.
Identifiers: LCCN 2016962326 | ISBN 9781532110467 (lib. bdg.) | ISBN 9781680788310 (ebook)
Subjects: LCSH: Wu, C.S. (Chien-Shiung), 1912-1997--Juvenile literature. | Nuclear physicists--United States--Biography--Juvenile literature. | Nuclear physicists--China--Biography--Juvenile literature. | Women physicists--Biography--Juvenile literature. | Chinese Americans--Biography--Juvenile literature.
Classification: DDC 530.92 [B]--dc23
LC record available at http://lccn.loc.gov/2016962326

# CONTENTS

# MADAME PHYSICIST

In October 1964, echoes of applause rang in Chien-Shiung Wu's ears as she stepped down from the stage at the Massachusetts Institute of Technology (MIT) auditorium. The diminutive, middle-aged woman wearing a *cheongsam*, a traditional Chinese dress, had just delivered an inspiring speech. She spoke to a large gathering of scientists, educators, students, and members of the media.

In a calm and confident manner, Wu stated, "I wonder whether the tiny atoms and nuclei, or the mathematical symbols, or the DNA molecules have any preference for either masculine or feminine treatment."[1]

Renowned nuclear physicist Chien-Shiung Wu was a strong advocate for women in science professions.

The audience at that symposium, Women and the Scientific Professions, was eager to hear more of what the famous physicist, dubbed the "Queen of Nuclear Research," had to say about American women in science and engineering.[2] The listeners wondered why resistance to women in science had not already been overcome by the second half of the twentieth century. Wu provided the answer.

"I sincerely doubt that any open-minded person really believes in the faulty notion that women have no intellectual

## What Is Physics?

Physics is the scientific study of how matter and energy act and interact with each other. The word *physics* comes from the Greek word *phusiké*, meaning "knowledge of nature." Physics involves the study of motion, force, heat, sound, electricity, magnetism, gravity, light and other forms of radiation, the structure and behavior of atoms, and more. The scope of exploration ranges from the tiniest subatomic particles to entire galaxies and beyond. Chemistry, biology, geology, astronomy, and even psychology are affected by principles that find their origins in physics.

Wu was a groundbreaking pioneer in the field of nuclear physics. All

matter, meaning any substance that has mass and occupies space, is composed of atoms. Nuclear physicists study the composition and forces at work within the nucleus at the center of an atom. The nucleus comprises protons and neutrons, and electrons move in wavelike fashion outside the nucleus. Owing to their electrical charges, protons and neutrons within the nucleus are inclined to fly apart, but they are bound together by a strong nuclear force. Scientists have discovered many applications for nuclear physics, including medicine, energy, geology, and weaponry.

capacity for science and technology," she asserted. "Nor do I believe that social and economic factors are the actual obstacles that prevent women's participation in the scientific and technical field. . . . The main stumbling block in the way of progress is and always has been unimpeachable tradition."[3]

Wu's words rang true with her distinguished audience: There was no acceptable reason for women to have fewer rights than men or to earn less respect when pursuing scientific advancements.

## Wu on Sexism

Wu's experiences as the leading female scientist among male nuclear physicists in the United States made her an outspoken voice on sexism in science. "It is shameful that there are so few women in science. . . . In China there are many, many women in physics," she told a *Newsweek* reporter in 1963. "There is a misconception in America that women scientists are all dowdy spinsters. This is the fault of men. In Chinese society, a woman is valued for what she is, and men encourage her [in her] accomplishments yet she remains eternally feminine."[4]

# OVERCOMING OBSTACLES

Chien-Shiung Wu (meaning "courageous hero" in Chinese) conquered the dual biases of sexism and anti-Asian sentiment in the United States during the 1940s and 1950s with hard work, determination, and remarkable problem-solving skills. Born in China, the world-renowned American nuclear physicist fought throughout her life to overcome prejudice against women and Asians. As an educator and an experimenter, Wu urged her

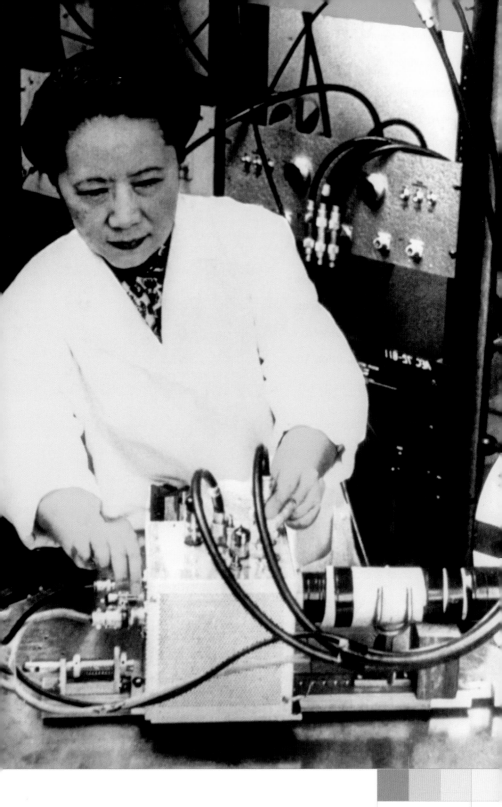

female students to embrace scientific study and research. She also spoke out against the discrimination women faced in the classroom and in the laboratory. Leaving her homeland and her family in China—many of whom she never saw again after sailing to the United States—Wu not only overcame discrimination but also showed the world that women and men are equal in the world of science.

## Anti-Asian Sentiment

Racism toward Asians in the United States began long before the Japanese bombing of Pearl Harbor on December 7, 1941, the event that dragged the United States into World War II (1939–1945). In the mid-nineteenth century, anti-Asian prejudice was common throughout the United States when Chinese immigrants began arriving for the California Gold Rush. A specially created foreign-miners' tax was imposed in California in 1852 to discriminate against Chinese miners. Two years later, the California Supreme Court barred Chinese people from testifying in court, making it virtually impossible to prosecute those who committed crimes against Chinese immigrants. Restrictive federal laws in the late 1800s limited and even prohibited the immigration of Chinese people. Anti-Asian prejudice extended to Japanese immigrants, who had initially been recruited to the Pacific Northwest in the 1880s to construct railroads. Tension arose over the possibility that they would take jobs and farmland from native-born Americans. As a result, in 1907, the United States and Japan made the Gentleman's Agreement, which suppressed Japanese immigration. After the bombing of Pearl Harbor, 120,000 Japanese Americans were ordered to leave their businesses and homes and were forced to live in internment camps situated largely in California.[5]

Wu began her career as an experimentalist at National Central University in Nanjing, China. Scientific research became her life's work.

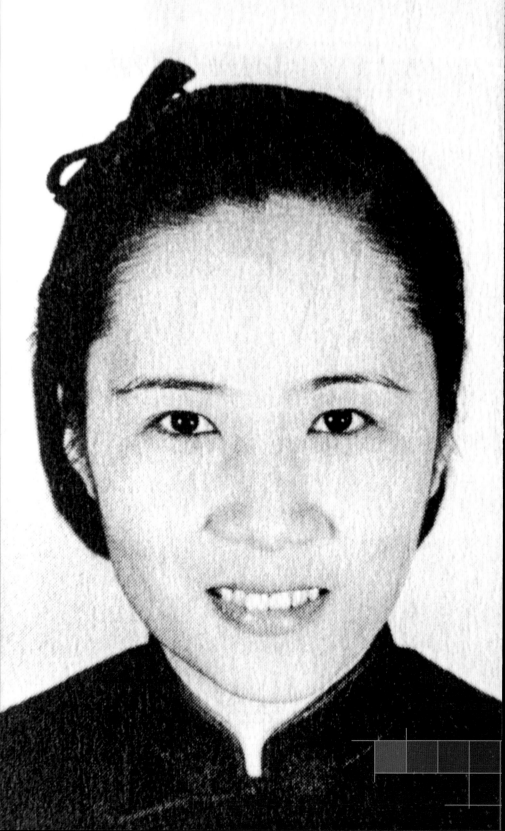

# TWO

# A STAR IS BORN

Chien-Shiung Wu was born on May 31, 1912, in Liuhe, China, approximately 30 miles (50 km) from the port city of Shanghai, China. Liuhe, located near the mouth of the Yangtze River, is a relatively small but important town in eastern China. Crowded with street commerce and ships, Liuhe is a major agricultural provider to the region and boasts a large fishing industry.

The China into which Chien-Shiung was born had recently undergone tremendous political upheaval. In 1911, a revolution toppled the centuries-old rule of dynasties and made the country a republic. Nevertheless, many traces of the old ways remained. In a nation where women were not treated as equals of men, however, Chien-Shiung benefited from life in a

From an early age, Chien-Shiung demonstrated intellectual curiosity and an aptitude for science.

progressive family in which education for both boys and girls was heartily encouraged.

## FAMILY LIFE

Chien-Shiung was one of three children in the Wu family. Her older brother, Chien-Ying, was born in 1909, and a younger brother, Chien-Hao, was born in 1920. Her father, Zong-Yi, was a forward-thinking, well-educated man who had studied engineering at Nanyang Public School in Shanghai. Zong-Yi possessed an unquenchable desire for knowledge and read extensively, particularly books and periodicals on human rights. Chien-Shiung's mother was Fan Fu-Hua.

Intelligent and curious, Chien-Shiung became the lucky beneficiary of Zong-Yi's passion for learning. The house was filled with books and magazines, which the father encouraged his children to read. Zong-Yi even read scientific articles aloud to his young daughter before she could read. Chien-Shiung was particularly captivated by the international news brought into the Wu household through her father's old radio. Above all, Zong-Yi wished to prepare his children for life in the modern world.

## EARLY EDUCATION

The first school Chien-Shiung attended was Ming De School, founded by her father. A strong advocate of women's education,

Zong-Yi converted a former temple into the girls' school and served as its principal. Attending the school was free for any girl, rich or poor. Courses included sewing, gardening, and other trades. Subjects such as mathematics, classical literature, Chinese culture, and history were also taught. At a time when women in China were still having their feet bound to symbolize status and beauty, Zong-Yi's girls' school amounted to a revolutionary departure from the past.

Chien-Shiung loved to learn and was a star pupil at Ming De School, supplemented by daily discussions at home with her father. A former engineer, Zong-Yi regaled his daughter with stories of scientific research and discovery. These early lessons in science laid the foundation for Chien-Shiung's groundbreaking accomplishments in later life.

In 1921, at age nine, Chien-Shiung graduated from

## Zong-Yi

The progressive ideas embraced by Chien-Shiung's father, Zong-Yi, were not welcome at Nanyang Public School, where he did his university studies. Zong-Yi and several friends transferred to Ai-Kuo ("love your country") Academy, as they were attracted by the academic freedom that flourished there. The campus buzzed with discussions about democracy and diversity. In 1909, Zong-Yi joined the Shanghai Merchant Corporation and studied military techniques. He and his associates played an important role in the success of the Shanghai Revolt that overthrew the emperor in 1911. A second revolution, to unseat the new acting president of China, failed, and Zong-Yi returned home to Liuhe. He worked as an engineer and followed his broad interests in hunting, singing, and reading poetry.

# Student Activist

While attending Soochow Girls High School, Chien-Shiung was urged by friends to lead an underground student movement to protest Japan's aggression. Chien-Shiung organized peaceful student strikes and boycotts of Japanese goods. As a university student in December 1932, Chien-Shiung, waving a Chinese flag, led a group of several hundred students in a demonstration at Chiang Kai-shek's presidential palace in Nanjing. Chiang Kai-shek, a military leader from the Kuomintang party who had helped overthrow the Qing Dynasty in 1911, had become president of the Chinese republic in 1925. The students demonstrating at the palace urged the government to declare war on Japan. The president met with the students, explaining the dangers of all-out conflict with the Japanese, and he agreed to do what he could. Dissatisfied with the leader's response, the students dispersed and went home.

her father's school. With no other schools in Liuhe, the Wu family was presented with a dilemma: Where could this bright, young girl continue her education? Zong-Yi consulted with his great-grandmother, the family matriarch. The older woman proclaimed Chien-Shiung should attend the best school possible.

Fortunately, Zong-Yi had a friend who taught at the Suzhou (Soochow in its anglicized form) Girls High School in Suzhou, a boarding school 50 miles (80 km) from Liuhe. The man promised to make sure Chien-Shiung's stay would be enjoyable, and in 1923, at age 11, the young girl left her hometown to continue her education.

The Soochow school had an excellent reputation. Famous scholars from around the world came to lecture at Soochow, and the school had many fine teachers. Soochow offered two types of classes: a teachers-in-training program and a general program for high school students. Chien-Shiung decided to enroll in the teachers-in-training program because the tuition was free, and she was guaranteed a teaching position after graduation.

Chien-Shiung emerged as an outstanding student, admired by teachers and fellow students alike. She studied hard and eagerly participated in classroom activities and discussions. She particularly enjoyed attending lectures offered at the school. Chien-Shiung befriended one lecturer, Hu Shih, a famous

Chien-Shiung's mentor, Hu Shih, recognized her extraordinary intellect and her determination to succeed.

Chinese philosopher and diplomat who would have a profound effect on the course of her life.

Soochow was a boarding school, and the girls from both programs lived in the same dormitory. In conversations with roommates, Chien-Shiung learned the program for regular high school students featured more science subjects than her teachers-in-training program. Eager to learn science, Chien-Shiung began borrowing her friends' textbooks in physics, chemistry, and math. While the others slept, she studied into the early morning hours, furthering her understanding of the world of science, particularly physics. She called this practice "self-learning," a habit she would continue the rest of her life.[1]

# THE COLLEGE YEARS

In 1929, Chien-Shiung graduated from high school with the highest grades in her class. Not surprisingly, she was accepted into the prestigious National Central University (NCU) in Nanjing, China, without having to take an entrance examination. Chien-Shiung wanted to study physics there but believed she didn't have a strong enough background in science or math to succeed at NCU. Instead, she enrolled at the National China College in Shanghai for a brief period and took courses in mathematics, history, sociology, and writing. Hu Shih, Wu's beloved lecturer at Soochow, was teaching at the National China College, and she became his favorite student.

Meanwhile, Chien-Shiung's father, Zong-Yi, encouraged his daughter to keep her sights on studying physics at NCU. "There's ample time to prepare yourself," he said.[2] Zong-Yi brought home books on advanced mathematics, chemistry, and physics. Wu spent the entire summer studying, increasing her knowledge of these subjects. "If it hadn't been for my father's encouragement, I would be teaching grade school somewhere in China now," she later said.[3]

Confident she had sufficiently prepared for the next phase of her education, Chien-Shiung entered NCU. She majored in mathematics as a freshman but switched to physics in her sophomore year. Chien-Shiung spent many hours in NCU's science laboratories developing the skills of an experimentalist: designing experiments and tests, recording data and results, making careful

## Campus Life at NCU

Throughout her career, Chien-Shiung was single-mindedly focused on learning. Though she did not participate in many extracurricular activities at NCU, former classmates recall she made new friends easily and was well liked by both male and female students. She had several close friends and especially enjoyed the company of those studying fine arts and humanities.

Chien-Shiung was a serious student and preferred to avoid distractions that interfered with her passion for physics, including romance. Her friends do not recall Wu having a steady boyfriend during her stay at NCU. At first, Wu shared a room with other students in the women's dormitory, but she later transferred to a single room to better focus on her studies. The small room was no larger than 100 square feet (9 sq m), and Wu often studied by candlelight after the dormitory electricity was shut off late at night.

Chien-Shiung was a role model for women in the male-dominated field of physics.

observations, and drawing well-founded conclusions. She studied the work of Marie Curie, the famous Polish-French physicist who conducted important work in radioactivity in the early 1900s. Some of Chien-Shiung's classmates said Curie was Chien-Shiung's role model.

## LAUNCHING A CAREER

Chien-Shiung graduated from NCU with honors in 1934. Her next stop was Zhejiang University as a teaching assistant.

There, the chair of the physics department, Zhang Shao-Zhong, asked Chien-Shiung if she wished to work in Academia Sinica ("Chinese Academy" in Latin) in Shanghai. Academia Sinica is a government-sponsored institution with distinguished physics and chemistry research departments. Chien-Shiung jumped at the opportunity and was once again exempted from taking the customary entrance exam.

Chien-Shiung left Zhejiang University after one year and joined the staff at Academia Sinica in 1935. Her adviser was Jing-Wei Gu, a female research professor who had earned a PhD from the University of Michigan in the United States. Chien-Shiung and Gu worked closely together in the lab, often laboring night and day under dim lighting.

Chien-Shiung desperately wanted to continue her physics studies, but there were no Chinese graduate

## The Turbulent Years

The political climate in China during Chien-Shiung's university years was threatening and uncertain. In September 1931, during Chien-Shiung's freshman year at NCU, Japan invaded the resource-rich Chinese province of Manchuria and established a pro-Japanese government there. The next year, Japan landed troops in Shanghai. The Chinese Army held off the attack in bloody combat, and a cease-fire finally ended the conflict. Chinese people, especially students, were outraged and demanded the Chinese government take swift action against Japan. The Chinese government under General Chiang Kai-shek, still struggling in its infancy, maintained a wait-and-see position, hoping war with Japan could be avoided. But by 1937, Japan capitalized on the perceived weakness of China and launched a full-scale invasion that would last for the duration of World War II.

schools that offered physics. Gu suggested her assistant study abroad. Chien-Shiung's teacher and mentor, Hu Shih, even made a special visit to Academia Sinica to offer his support.

Funding for the venture to study overseas came in the summer of 1936 from Zong-Yi's brother, Zhuo-Zhi, a wealthy businessman. Chien-Shiung was accepted at the University of Michigan and began making plans for the long journey across the Pacific Ocean. She planned to make the crossing with Dong Ruo-Fen, a female friend who had lived in Chien-Shiung's hometown. Dong would also be attending the University of Michigan.

Chien-Shiung's ultimate goal was to obtain her PhD and quickly return to China to serve her country. Things couldn't have worked out more differently.

Chien-Shiung's career ambitions led her to the United States to continue her education, forever changing the course of her life.

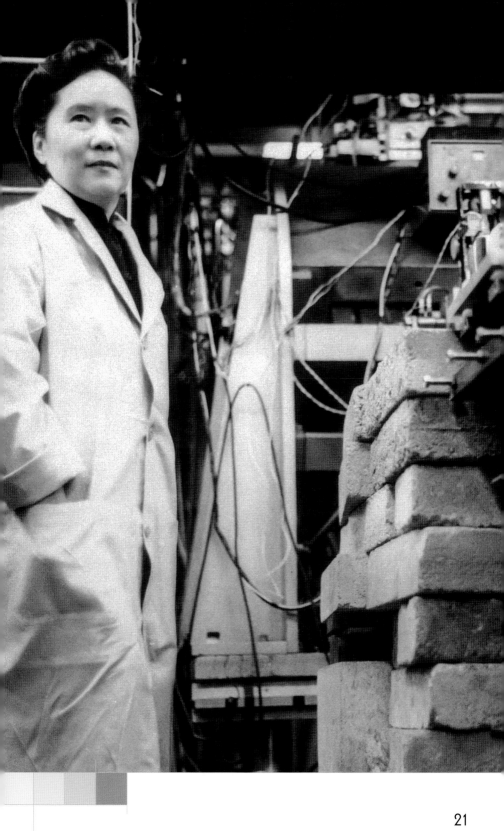

# THREE

# COMING TO THE UNITED STATES

In August 1936, Chien-Shiung Wu's family assembled at Huang Pu Bund, a waterfront area in central Shanghai. They had gathered to see her off on the journey to the United States. Standing on the deck of the ocean liner *President Hoover*, Wu and her traveling companion, Dong Ruo-Fen, sadly waved good-bye to their loved ones.

Little could anyone there have suspected that Wu's trip to obtain a degree in the United States would last 37 years. She would never see her father and mother again.

## ARRIVING AT BERKELEY

As the *President Hoover* made its way eastward across the vast Pacific Ocean, Wu wasn't sure what to expect about her

Wu left her home and family in China to pursue a graduate degree in the United States.

new life in the United States. She spoke English, but not very well. She knew a little about US culture from magazines and newspapers and from what her father had told her about the United States and Western democracy. Despite her limited knowledge, Wu was anticipating a rewarding experience in her new home.

Wu's first stop was San Francisco, California. She planned to stay for a week visiting a friend, Lin, whose husband, Guo, taught nearby at the University of California, Berkeley. After the brief visit, Wu and Dong would resume their trip eastward to the University of Michigan.

Wu was introduced to Victor Yang, the president of Berkeley's Chinese Students' Association. In turn, Yang introduced Wu to a new arrival at the university, physics graduate student Luke Yuan. Yuan was the grandson of Yuan Shikai, a famous Chinese general who had been elected the first formal president of the new Republic of China in 1915. Shikai tried unsuccessfully to restore a dynasty in China, and his short-lived reign lasted only four months.

Although traditional Chinese custom dictates that a person's name be represented by the family name followed by the individual's first name, Wu elected to follow Western style. As such, she became known as Chien-Shiung Wu instead of Wu

Wu was impressed by Berkeley's research facilities and faculty, including Ernest Lawrence, *left*, J. Robert Oppenheimer, and the cyclotron.

Chien-Shiung as she had been known in China. Luke Yuan, born Yuan Chia-Liu, made the same change upon his arrival at Berkeley and also chose an English first name in place of his Chinese name. Yuan accompanied Wu on a tour of the Berkeley campus. The cutting-edge experimental equipment in the physics department, especially the large cyclotron, particularly impressed Wu. A cyclotron is a machine used in nuclear physics experiments that accelerates charged particles within an electric field.

The physics department at Berkeley boasted a top-notch staff of teachers and researchers. Ernest Lawrence, only 35 years old, had built the cyclotron Wu admired. J. Robert Oppenheimer, 28 years old, was teaching bold, new theories about the behavior of atoms and subatomic particles. Oppenheimer would later become famous for developing the atomic bomb through the US government's Manhattan Project. The idea of studying with and working alongside such top young scientists appealed to the 24-year-old Wu.

While chatting with students at Berkeley, Wu was shocked to learn women were not allowed to use the front entrance at the University of Michigan's new student center. She was surprised such discrimination against women existed in the United States. Wu wondered how she could attend a school where she would have to settle for second-class treatment.

Wu was also dismayed to hear Michigan had more than 600 Chinese students. She wasn't keen on the idea of having traveled all the way to the United States only to spend most of her time with other Chinese students. Before her weeklong visit had ended, Wu made a life-changing decision: she would not go to Michigan but would stay at Berkeley instead.

Wu met with the chair of the physics department, Raymond Birge. Criticized for discriminating against foreigners, Birge had nonetheless built Berkeley's physics department into one of the world's finest. In their meeting, Wu impressed Birge with her intelligence and ambition. Recognizing her talent and potential, Birge agreed to accept her into the graduate program even though the school year had already started at Berkeley.

When Wu informed her travel mate that she was staying at Berkeley, her friend was angered at the sudden change of plans.

## The Cyclotron

Cyclotrons are often called particle accelerators or atom smashers. These machines use electric power to accelerate the charged particles of an atom in a spiral path at superhigh speeds. The particles are then sent crashing into the nuclei of atoms. The collision produces radioactive isotopes that can be used in medicine, industry, and scientific research, including the study of nuclear reactions inside stars.

Protons are gathered in the cyclotron and placed in a round vacuum chamber that is surrounded by large, powerful electromagnets. An electric current is applied to accelerate the protons. The protons gain energy from the current and start to travel around in circles, moving faster and faster along the walls of the vacuum chamber. When the protons reach a certain speed, they are released out of the chamber and directed so they bombard the atoms of a given element. The atoms are disintegrated and form, in some cases, entirely new elements. Hundreds of radioactive isotopes have been discovered with the cyclotron.

In 1931, Lawrence and his Berkeley graduate student M. Stanley Livingston built the first cyclotron capable of accelerating particles to sufficiently high speeds. One year later, the two men began drawing up plans for a larger, more powerful cyclotron. It was this larger machine that impressed Wu on her tour of the Berkeley campus in 1936.

Dong headed to Michigan alone and studied chemistry, but the two women's friendship was never the same.

## THE BERKELEY YEARS

Wu moved into International House (i-House), a dormitory for foreign and US graduate students. Wu's initial encounter with her new surroundings went poorly. Arriving in the cafeteria for her first breakfast at i-House, Wu expected to find her usual bowl of rice. Instead, she found nothing but unfamiliar foods, all of which had to be ordered by name—a daunting task for a young woman who spoke limited English. Frustrated, Wu left the cafeteria without eating. Later that day, she journeyed off campus and was relieved to find a shop serving spring rolls and tea.

Wu also met a new friend on her first day, Ursula Schaefer, a German student who was studying history. Schaefer loved Chinese food, and like Wu, she didn't care at all for the cafeteria fare at i-House. The two women soon found a Chinese restaurant called the Tea Garden. The kind owner allowed the students to enjoy a sumptuous dinner anytime they wanted for only 25 cents. Wu frequently ate there with Ursula, Luke Yuan, and Willis Lamb, who would later marry Schaefer.

Wu and Schaefer became fast friends, and their friendship would last their lifetimes. Schaefer took Wu to the opera, and Wu introduced Schaefer to the culture of San Francisco's Chinatown. Wu and Schaefer enjoyed learning about each other's cultures. To display her pride in her Chinese heritage, Wu always wore the traditional Chinese high-collared dress called the *cheongsam*, or *qipao*.

Spending time in San Francisco's Chinatown allowed Wu to connect with familiar aspects of Chinese culture.

Shortly after Wu settled into daily campus life, her favorite teacher, Hu Shih, visited her at Berkeley. He was elated to learn his prize student was following her dream with diligence and commitment.

Wu's intelligence, enthusiasm, and cheery disposition made her a popular figure on the Berkeley campus—a star student admired by professors and other students alike. Ursula Schaefer remarked that her friend had a "smile that brought the sunlight right into your lap."[1] Her brilliant teacher, Robert Oppenheimer, praised her work and her determination to succeed.

Wu and Yuan applied for scholarships at the end of their first year, but both were awarded only small stipends despite being recommended for fellowships by the physics department. At the time, there was considerable prejudice against Asians in US universities, and Berkeley was no exception. Yuan, disappointed, applied to the California Institute of Technology (Caltech) in Southern California. Caltech president Robert Millikan gladly offered the talented physicist a scholarship and arranged for Yuan's immediate acceptance. Millikan had won the Nobel Prize in Physics in 1923 for his work on the charge of electrons.

The separation from Yuan, by now a special friend to Wu, was followed by news in July 1937 that Japan had invaded China. Wu would be cut off from all communication with her family.

Despite Wu's popularity within the physics department, her scholarship opportunities were limited because of her Chinese heritage.

She had no way of knowing about their safety and realized she could not return home until the war was over.

## PHD AND BEYOND

Wu finished her second year with outstanding grades and prepared to work on her PhD dissertation. Ernest Lawrence became her official adviser, but her real adviser was Emilio Segrè, a prominent Italian physicist who had worked on nuclear experiments in the 1920s.

In 1938, Lawrence directed Wu's first doctoral experiment. The purpose of the experiment was to study the energy given off when a particle goes through matter. The following year, Segrè directed Wu's experiments on beta particles, the radioactive fragments emitted when a uranium molecule splits; this process is known as uranium fission. Wu later used the results of her findings when she participated in developing the atomic bomb.

Both Lawrence and Segrè praised Wu's precise and accurate style of research and experimentation. They hailed her work ethic and admired her total devotion to her tasks. Wu often worked in her laboratory into the late hours of the night. The physics department, concerned for Wu's safety when returning to i-House, arranged for a fellow student, Robert Wilson, to

Wu was taught by the most respected nuclear physicists in the world, including Emilio Segrè.

drive her home each night. Wilson, who also liked to keep late hours, would come by Wu's lab at 3:00 or 4:00 a.m., saying, "Miss Wu, it's time for you to go home."[2]

Despite Wu's intense focus on her work, she could not detach herself from world affairs. In China, Japanese troops had captured several large cities in 1937 and 1938, including Shanghai and Nanjing. Japanese soldiers killed tens of thousands of Chinese civilians. Was her family among those who had been murdered, she wondered?

Wu received her PhD in physics in 1940. She remained at Berkeley for two years as a postdoctoral research assistant and became an expert in nuclear fission, the process of splitting an atom's nucleus. Oppenheimer referred to her as the authority on the subject. Wu also continued working with Segrè. By 1941, she was lecturing outside the university, and her reputation began spreading rapidly.

## Nobel Prize Winner

Emilio Segrè was born in 1905 in Tivoli, Italy. He earned his PhD in physics in 1928 at the University of Rome under the famous physicist Enrico Fermi, who went on to win the 1938 Nobel Prize in Physics. After serving as director of the physics laboratory at the University of Palermo, Segrè came to Berkeley in 1938 as a research associate in the radiation laboratory. In 1943, he became a group leader in work on the atomic bomb. After the war, Segrè returned to Berkeley as a professor of physics, serving until 1972. Segrè helped discover the elements technetium, astatine, and plutonium-239. He was awarded the 1959 Nobel Prize in Physics for his discovery of what is known as the antiproton, which in simple terms is a proton with a negative charge.

# ATOMIC
# ACTIVITY

## ENERGY THROUGH DISINTEGRATION

Researchers have discovered 118 elements. Elements are substances consisting of only one kind of atom that cannot be broken down into a simpler form. Elements make up all matter on Earth. For example, water is a combination of the elements hydrogen and oxygen. Elements are composed of atoms. In turn, atoms are made up of three particles: protons, neutrons, and electrons. The protons and neutrons are in the nucleus of an atom. For most elements, the number of protons equals the number of neutrons and electrons. An element that gains or loses neutrons, becoming a heavier or lighter version of itself, is called an isotope. Sometimes, to reach stability, isotopes with an unstable nucleus cast off neutrons. Such isotopes are called radioactive isotopes.

The energy produced by radioactivity, called radiation, can change the cells in the human body and cause diseases such as cancer. But science has also used radiation for many beneficial purposes. X-ray machines, equipment-sterilization procedures, nuclear medicine, and energy generation all use radiation safely. Many common, everyday objects and materials, such as cat litter, fluorescent lights, Brazil nuts, and even bananas, emit small, harmless amounts of radiation.

Unstable isotopes spontaneously decompose by casting off neutrons to reach stability. An element's radioactivity is measured by how quickly its isotopes decay over time.

RADIOACTIVE ENERGY

PARTICLE

RADIOACTIVE ATOM

# FOUR

# GOING EAST

During her postdoctoral research at Berkeley in 1941, Wu's adviser, Lawrence, encouraged her to take a break from her work and tour the East Coast. Since arriving in the United States in 1936, Wu had not traveled outside of California. The trip would be an ideal opportunity to meet new people and learn more about US culture and history.

Wu departed San Francisco by train in April and headed to the Midwest, making stops in Chicago, Illinois, and Saint Louis, Missouri. The next month, she arrived in Washington, DC, where she attended a meeting of the American Physical Society. Oppenheimer, Lawrence, and Segrè also attended. Wu enjoyed socializing with her professors away from the confines of the Berkeley physics laboratories. When the meetings ended, Wu

After spending nearly five years at Berkeley, Wu had a chance to visit other US states in 1941.

visited New York City and Boston, Massachusetts. During her extensive travels, Wu visited several universities and met other physicists. Her outstanding reputation as a top-notch physicist was quickly growing.

## NEWLYWEDS ON THE MOVE

Despite Wu's stellar performance at Berkeley and her blossoming stature, the university would not hire her for a faculty position. At the time, this was not unusual, as most top research universities in the United States did not hire female professors. In addition, anti-Asian sentiment on the West Coast had reached a fever pitch. Since the Japanese bombing of Pearl Harbor on December 7, 1941, the United States was at war with Japan. Tens of thousands of Japanese Americans were placed in internment camps, and though Wu was Chinese, many people considered any Asian a risk to national security. Ironically, China had been fighting Japan longer than the United States had.

After several years of a deepening romance while they were in different locations, Wu and Luke Yuan were married in Pasadena, California, in May 1942. The wedding was held at the home of Robert Millikan, the president of Caltech who had offered Yuan a scholarship in 1937. Millikan had been Yuan's thesis adviser.

As Wu and Yuan pondered their future, Yuan decided to accept a position designing radar for the US Department of Defense at RCA Laboratories in Princeton, New Jersey. Wu took a teaching job with Smith College in Northampton, Massachusetts. Though Smith was not a research university as was Berkeley, she accepted the job to be near her husband on the East Coast. The newlyweds met in New York City on weekends.

Wu was an able and admired assistant professor, but she regretted Smith College did not have the financial resources to fund her research. She was also sad to be apart from Yuan except for the few short hours they shared on weekends. Furthermore, Wu missed her Berkeley associates, many of whom had already joined

## Father of the Atomic Bomb

J. Robert Oppenheimer was born in 1904 in New York, New York. At age 18, he went to Harvard University, where he developed a passion for physics. Oppenheimer later studied at Cambridge University in England and then at Göttingen University in Germany. By the time he returned to the United States, he was a widely respected physicist. After the start of World War II, the US government selected Oppenheimer to lead a team of scientists in the Manhattan Project. The goal of the program was to find military uses for atomic energy. In 1941, Oppenheimer gathered his team at Berkeley to begin work on the atomic bomb. After the bomb was used against Japan, Oppenheimer expressed regret about its use for a deadly purpose. In a meeting with President Harry S. Truman in 1946, Oppenheimer remarked, "Mr. President, I have blood on my hands."[1]

Oppenheimer to work on the Manhattan Project. Though an expert on fission, Wu had not been asked to join the team.

## MAKING HISTORY

While teaching at Smith College, Wu was largely disconnected from the latest developments in physics and the scientists making new advances in the field. To keep abreast of the news, she attended various conferences. At a conference in Boston, Wu met Lawrence, her former teacher from Berkeley. Lawrence, a brilliant experimentalist, sensed his former associate was dissatisfied with her current situation.

"Are you happy not doing any experiments?" Lawrence asked.

"I feel sort of out of the way," Wu replied.[2]

Lawrence was aware that many of the nation's top physicists were serving in government defense jobs and that universities needed scientists, male or female. He immediately wrote letters to several major universities, recommending they hire Wu. The response was overwhelming: eight universities, including Princeton, Harvard, Columbia, and MIT, offered her a position. At the time, several of these schools did not even admit female undergraduates. Nonetheless, in 1943, at age 31, Wu accepted the offer from Princeton and became the first female professor in the school's history. Wu's students were US Navy officers sent to Princeton to learn physics. Most importantly, Wu and Yuan could finally be together.

# WORKING ON
# THE MANHATTAN PROJECT

Wu's stay at Princeton was short-lived. Several months after she began her professorship, Lawrence recommended her for an interview at Columbia University in New York City and

## The Manhattan Project

By 1939, physicists knew a fission chain reaction could produce enormous power and be used in a weapon. That same year, Enrico Fermi began his work on producing a chain reaction. US physicists were in a race against time, as they learned German physicists had discovered the secret of how to split a uranium atom. The famous scientist Albert Einstein, who had left Germany in 1933 because of the strengthening Nazi movement, was now living in the United States. At the urging of Hungarian physicist Leo Szilard, Einstein sent a letter to President Franklin D. Roosevelt informing him that the Germans could be developing a bomb. The letter advised taking immediate action to begin work on an atomic bomb in the United States, and Roosevelt agreed.

In February 1940, the federal government allocated $6,000 to begin research on the bomb, with additional funding provided in subsequent months. In late 1941, the project was given its code name: the Manhattan Project. Research was based at several universities, including Columbia, Berkeley, and the University of Chicago. Nuclear facilities were built in Oak Ridge, Tennessee, and Hanford, Washington. The main assembly facility was set up in Los Alamos, New Mexico. Oppenheimer supervised the entire program. In total, nearly $2 billion ($34.5 billion in today's dollars) was spent on developing the atomic bomb, and the project employed more than 120,000 people.[3]

## Blackboard Interview

Wu's interview for the job at Columbia University's Division of War Research took place in an office in the jet propulsion department. In the course of a day, two physicists peppered Wu with questions about advanced topics in physics. Because the atomic bomb project was top-secret, they were careful not to reveal what they were working on. There was one break in their secrecy, however; they had forgotten to erase the blackboards in the room. At the end of the day, they asked, "Now, Miss Wu, do you know anything about what we're doing here?" "I'm sorry," she smiled, "but if you wanted me not to know what you're doing, you should have cleaned the blackboards." The two men laughed and said, "Since you already know what's going on, can you start tomorrow morning?"[4]

its new Division of War Research. She impressed the interviewers, and in March 1944, Wu, a noncitizen, received special permission and top-secret clearance to join Columbia as a senior scientist working on the Manhattan Project. She was elated to resume her physics research and contribute to the Allied war effort and, in so doing, help end China's suffering at Japan's hands.

By this time, there had been significant progress on the technology behind the atomic bomb. Scientists, however, faced two main obstacles: producing enough uranium-235 for the bomb and developing a method to make nuclear fission self-sustaining through a chain reaction process. The process began with the splitting of an atom's nucleus, after which the subatomic particles would then shoot into other atoms, splitting them apart as well. This ongoing process resulted in enormous amounts of energy being released. The dilemma for Wu and

Wu at Columbia University

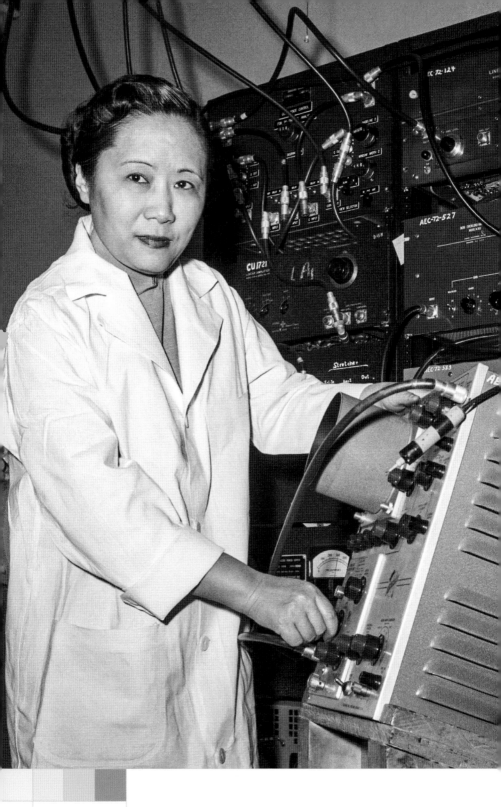

# SCIENCE
# SPOTLIGHT

## FISSION VS. FUSION

Energy is released when the nucleus of an atom either splits or is fused with another nucleus. In nuclear fission, a large atom is split into two or more smaller atoms. Nuclear fusion occurs when two small atoms, such as hydrogen, fuse together to create a larger atom. Fusion occurs in stars, such as the sun, where temperatures can be in the millions of degrees.

The energy released by fission is much greater than that released in most chemical reactions, but it is lower than the energy released by fusion. Nuclear fusion can produce four times the energy produced by fission. Both types of reactions have been used in nuclear weapons. The atomic bomb is a fission bomb. Fission bombs usually use uranium or plutonium as the fuel. The hydrogen bomb, in contrast to the atomic bomb, is a fission bomb with a fusion bomb inside. The fission bomb produces extremely high pressures and temperatures that bring nuclei very close together, resulting in a fusion reaction. The fuel in fusion bombs is commonly two isotopes of hydrogen, deuterium and tritium.

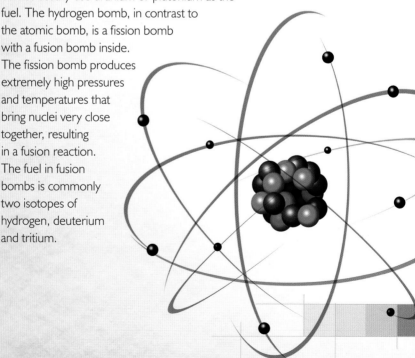

Wu's expertise aided the research on the atomic bomb at the Hanford Reactor in eastern Washington.

others was how to create conditions under which the process could continue on its own.

First, Wu helped solve the problem of how to generate uranium-235. Working in a converted automobile warehouse near Columbia University, Wu used a very complex process called gas diffusion to separate uranium metal into uranium-235 (U-235) and uranium-238 (U-238) isotopes. The numbers 235 and 238 refer to the number of protons and neutrons in each of these common isotopes of uranium. U-238 is three neutrons heavier than U-235. Both of these isotopes have very long lifetimes, meaning they are very stable. Uranium mined from the earth is composed mostly of U-238, with a small amount of U-235. Wu's process effectively extracted the scarce U-235 from the more plentiful U-238.

Meanwhile, Enrico Fermi, the Italian-born physicist and Columbia professor known for his work with uranium and nuclear fission, was in Washington State working on solving the chain reaction problem. On September 27, 1944, Fermi started up the Hanford Reactor in eastern Washington. The chain reaction began well but stopped after several hours. It then started again after a few more hours. Fermi believed a by-product of the fission process was causing the stop-and-start problem, but he wasn't exactly sure what was wrong.

According to the story, someone—perhaps Wu's professor, Segrè—told Fermi to "ask Miss Wu."[5] Just as had happened with the uranium separation problem, Wu had the answer. During her PhD work on fission at Berkeley, Wu had discovered that a gas called xenon was produced during the fission process. She informed Fermi that xenon was the cause of the faulty chain

The power within a nuclear fission bomb is generated by successive chain reactions of energetic neutrons breaking nuclei.

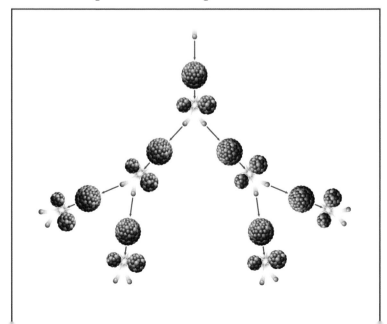

reaction. Fermi made the necessary adjustments to eliminate the xenon buildup, and work on the atomic bomb proceeded.

In July 1945, the bomb was successfully tested at the top-secret weapons laboratory in Los Alamos, New Mexico. The following month, an atomic bomb was dropped on each of the cities Hiroshima and Nagasaki in Japan, leading to the Japanese surrender and the end of World War II.

# AFTER THE WAR

Several weeks after Japan surrendered, Wu received a note from her family in China. The news was good: her parents and her brothers were well. They had not been harmed during the violence in their country. Wu's father, Zong-Yi, had emerged as a national hero for his role in the Chinese war effort. The former engineer had supervised the construction of the Burma Road, which ran

## Truman Tested

The United States successfully tested its atomic bomb on July 16, 1945, in the desert near Alamogordo, New Mexico. Would the Americans unleash its incredible power to end the war with Japan? First, the Allies demanded an immediate surrender by Japan's leaders. Refusal would result in complete destruction, the demand warned. Japanese military commanders rejected the proposal. Reluctantly, President Harry S. Truman made the decision to use the fearsome new weapon. Truman had been president for less than four months following the sudden death of President Franklin D. Roosevelt in April. On August 6, 1945, the B-29 Superfortress *Enola Gay* dropped an atomic bomb on the city of Hiroshima. Still, Japan's military commanders refused to surrender. Three days later, a second bomb was dropped on Nagasaki. On August 14, Japan finally surrendered. More than 300,000 people died in the two bombings or from their effects.[6]

Nuclear weapons generate giant mushroom clouds consisting of hot, radioactive gases.

from eastern Burma (now Myanmar) to Kunming in southwest China. The one-lane, 717-mile (1,154-km) highway was a vital supply route used by the Allies to move food and resources into China's interior.[7]

During their years working on the East Coast, Wu and Yuan dreamed of returning to their homeland as soon as possible. With the war over, perhaps the time had come to realize their dream. But by the end of 1945, China was on the verge of civil war. The nationalist Kuomintang government under Chiang Kai-shek and the Chinese Communist Party led by Mao Zedong were engaged in a bitter struggle for political and military control of China.

Wu and Yuan believed it was too dangerous to return home and decided to remain in the United States until things in China calmed down. Wu was deeply troubled by the situation. "It is just heartbreaking to think of the stupidity going on in our country," she wrote to a friend.[8]

Though disappointed, Wu remained focused on her work and began planning her next project. This time she would confirm an important theory and provide nuclear physics with one of its most significant breakthroughs.

## Birds of a Feather

Luke Yuan, Wu's husband, was born in 1912 in Anyang, China. He attended the Academy of Modern Learning, studying physics and mathematics. He later attended the College of Industry and Commerce, majoring in engineering. In 1932, he earned his master's degree from Yenching University in Beijing. Several years later, Yenching's president, Leighton Stuart, asked Yuan if he wanted to apply for a scholarship at the University of California, Berkeley. Yuan was awarded the scholarship in 1936 and traveled by boat to San Francisco with only $40 to his name.[9] After receiving his PhD at Caltech and launching his career, Yuan became an authority on designing particle accelerators. He was a skilled experimentalist, and it was not uncommon for him to show up in Wu's lab after completing his workweek to assist Wu and her students. Following his retirement in 1979, Yuan founded the National Synchrotron Radiation Research Center in Taiwan. He died while visiting Beijing in 2003 at the age of 90.

# CHAPTER FIVE

# BETA DECAY

A fter the war ended in the fall of 1945, most wartime research stopped. Wu was one of the few Manhattan Project physicists asked to remain at Columbia University after the war. She was given the position of research professor, and most importantly, she had access to the university's excellent research facilities.

In February 1947, Wu and Yuan welcomed a new addition to the family when their son, Vincent, was born. The couple hired a nanny to care for Vincent, enabling Wu to maintain her demanding work schedule, researching and teaching at Columbia. Yuan, who had moved from RCA Laboratories to Princeton University as a research assistant in 1946, left Princeton in 1949 and took a position at Brookhaven National

Wu's significant contribution to the Manhattan Project enhanced her fame and advanced her career.

Laboratory on Long Island, New York. The couple bought a house on Long Island, and Wu also got an apartment near Columbia in New York City. She was ready to take on her next research project.

## Physicists' Son

Wu's only child, Vincent, was born in February 1947. With both parents fully engaged in their careers, Vincent attended a boarding school on Long Island for the first through fourth grades. He spent weekends with his parents at their apartment near Columbia University. Vincent did the rest of his schooling in New York City, except for eighth grade. He spent that year at a French boarding school while his father was on sabbatical in Europe. "It was an okay way to grow up," Vincent later recalled, though a former student of Wu's observed, "Her son would call and say he was hungry. He'd call and call."[1] On his own much of the time, Vincent learned to do his homework and cook for himself. Wu's students recalled how once, wanting their demanding professor to leave them alone in the lab for a few hours, they gave Wu two tickets so she could take Vincent to a children's movie. They thought they had secured some uninterrupted time in which to work, only to see a smiling Wu walk back into the lab, saying, "I sent him to the movie with the nursemaid."[2]

# RADIOACTIVE DECAY

When the nucleus of an atom emits radiation, the process is called radioactive decay. There are three main types of radioactive decay, depending on the isotope. Alpha decay occurs when there are too many protons in a nucleus. The element will emit radiation in the form of positively charged particles called alpha particles. Each alpha particle consists of two protons and two neutrons. In gamma decay, high-energy electromagnetic radiation is emitted from the element. There is no change in the number of protons or neutrons in the nucleus. Beta decay occurs when there are too many neutrons in a nucleus. A neutron can be thought of as a combination of an electron and a proton. Sometimes a neutron will decay into a proton, an electron, and another particle. When this occurs, the atom changes into another element. Wu decided beta decay would be her next research focus.

In 1934, Enrico Fermi had published an article on his theory on beta decay, predicting how the atom's nucleus would act during the process. Fermi believed electrons would be ejected from the atom's nucleus very rapidly. Scientists around the

Wu modified the standard spectrometer to conduct her work on beta decay.

world, however, had conducted experiments that did not confirm Fermi's theory. Their findings showed electrons coming out of the nucleus had much less energy than Fermi claimed. Wu accepted Fermi's theory and wanted to know why the other scientists were getting results that failed to prove his theory.

The physicists working on beta decay used a device called a spectrometer to measure the speed and energy of charged particles. Radioactive materials were mounted inside the device to provide a source of beta electrons. The source needed to be small enough to fit inside the spectrometer and also be capable of producing many electrons. To meet both conditions, scientists covered a slide with a thick film of radioactive material. But Wu believed it was the thick, uneven material that caused the electrons to lose speed and energy.

Wu began work on the problem in 1949. She decided not to use the same type of spectrometer the other physicists had used in their beta decay experiments. Instead, she redesigned an old spectrometer that had been put into storage. Wu adapted the device so it could accommodate thinner sources of radioactive materials.

Wu next made a thin and uniform source of radioactive materials. To do so, she added a few drops of a chemical solution resembling detergent to a bucket of water, which

Both scientific understanding and mechanical aptitude contributed to Wu's successes as a researcher.

then spread to form a thin film. She scooped up the film with a special copper tool and placed a drop of radioactive solution on the film. The radioactive material spread over the film thinly and uniformly. When the film dried, it was used as the source material in the spectrometer.

Each time Wu ran the beta decay experiment, her results supported Fermi's theory. Other scientists tried the experiment with thin and uniform source material and confirmed Fermi had been correct all along. Wu's work solved a problem that had stumped scientists for many years. This new knowledge led to other breakthroughs in physics in subsequent years. Wu's groundbreaking experiment established her as one of the world's premier authorities on beta decay and further cemented her reputation as an outstanding physics experimentalist. Wu continued working on beta decay until 1952.

## GOING HOME?

In 1949, the Communist Party seized power in China. At approximately this time, Wu's alma mater, NCU, offered both Wu and Yuan teaching positions. A move home would enable Wu to live and work with her husband and return to the family she had not seen for many years. As attractive as the offer seemed, Wu refused. Officials at the university gave the couple an additional year to conclude their work commitments in the United States and then come to China.

Meanwhile, the United States was not granting reentry visas to people visiting communist nations. If Wu and Yuan returned to China, they might not

### Beta Decay Expert

By the early 1950s, Wu had become the undisputed world authority on beta decay, and she openly discussed her passion for the subject. "To me, beta decay was still like a dear old friend," she said. "There would always be a place in my heart reserved especially for it."[3] Wu later coauthored Beta Decay, a textbook that has become a standard reference book on the subject. She wrote the book with physicist Steven Moszkowski of the University of California, Los Angeles.

Wu was recognized for her contributions to the Manhattan Project as one of *Mademoiselle* magazine's Young Women of the Year in 1946.

be allowed back into the United States. Wu asked her father, Zong-Yi, for advice. As desperately as he wanted to see his daughter, Zong-Yi advised Wu not to return at that time, citing his country's unstable political climate. Furthermore, Wu and

## "Dragon Lady"

As a teacher, Wu earned a reputation as a tough taskmaster among her students. Wu often asked her students to work late on weekdays and weekends. She became disappointed and angry if they failed to live up to her standards.

"It was very exciting," said Noemie Koller, one of Wu's graduate students. "But she was rough— very demanding. She pushed the students until they did it right. . . . She was never satisfied. She wanted people to work late at night, early in the morning, all day Saturday, all day Sunday, to do things faster, to never take time off."[4] Emilio Segrè, Wu's teacher-adviser at Berkeley remembered, "She is a slave driver. . . . She is the image of the militant woman so well known in Chinese literature as either empress or mother."[5]

Some of Wu's students nicknamed her the "Dragon Lady," a reference to the sinister Chinese woman who appeared in a popular newspaper comic strip of the time, *Terry and the Pirates*.[6] The students used the name affectionately, because they knew how much she wanted them to thrive and succeed under her guidance.

In the end, Wu's students considered her a beloved and trusted mentor. "She cared about our lives and relationships, even wrote to our parents to relate good news on our progress and achievements," said Koller. "She opened for us the doors of the physics community, inspired us with the highest professional standards, endowed our advisor-student relationship with grace, love and affection, showered us with friendship, encouragement, nurturing and continuous support long, long after we had left her laboratory."[7]

Yuan wanted Vincent to grow up in a democratic country, not a communist one. The couple remained in the United States and became naturalized US citizens in 1954.

# A STEP UP

Wu was promoted to associate professor at Columbia University in 1952, earning her an increase in pay and granting her tenure by adding teaching on top of her research activities. She continued her beta decay research, taught a course in nuclear physics, and served as adviser to several graduate students. Wu worked hard, often putting in 12 to 14 hours each day. Her routine started at approximately 8:00 a.m. After a full day of teaching and conducting research, she remained in the laboratory until 7:00 or 8:00 at night, and often until midnight.

Wu was a dedicated and tenacious teacher-researcher, and she expected similar dedication from her students. Although she could be stern and demanding, she was known to be fair. Just as she did for herself, Wu set lofty standards for her students and placed high expectations on them. She spoke enthusiastically with them about physics and other matters, and she built close-knit research teams whose members worked well together. Despite Wu's no-nonsense approach, students recognized and appreciated her personal warmth and her generous investment in their development as scientists. By the mid-1950s, Wu had seemingly reached the pinnacle of success in the world of physics. In actuality, she was just getting started.

# FUTURE
# TECH

## BETA DECAY IN MEDICINE

In recent decades, beta decay has been widely used in the field of oncology, the study of cancerous tumors. A positron emission tomography scan, popularly known as a PET scan, is an imaging technique that distributes a radioactive tracer in a patient's body to identify diseased areas. The tracer collects in areas where higher levels of certain chemicals suggest tumors might be present.

Radionuclide therapy, or radiotherapy, is a form of cancer treatment that also uses beta decay. The radiation released by beta decay helps weaken or destroy cancer cells in the human body. Drugs containing radioactive isotopes are introduced into a patient by injection into a vein or are taken orally in pill form. These drugs are called radiopharmaceuticals. The drugs travel through the body and build up in the area where cancer cells are present. As the radioactive atoms decay, they release beta particles that attack nearby cancer cells.

Scientists have discovered some isotopes are more effective on certain types of cancer than others. Phosphorus-32, an isotope of the element phosphorus, is used to treat hollow brain tumors, killing the tumor without harming the healthy parts of the brain. Iodine-131 is often used to treat thyroid cancer, and it is frequently used after thyroid cancer surgery to kill any cancer cells that remain.

Radioisotopes can be manufactured for use as chemical markers within a patient's body. These isotopes show up on scans and are useful in both diagnosing and treating cancer.

# SIX

# PARITY BREAKTHROUGH

W u had solved the great mystery of beta decay, and in so doing, she continued to gain the respect of other prominent physicists. Following her success in proving Fermi's theory, Wu spent 1952 to 1956 looking for new challenges in the field of nuclear physics. In May 1956, her quest ended with a knock on the door.

## LEE, YANG, AND PARITY

Tsung-Dao Lee, a Chinese-American physicist at Columbia, came to Wu's office at Columbia's Pupin Laboratories. Lee, who worked in a lab several floors below, came to his colleague for advice. He knew of her cutting-edge research in beta decay, as well as her well-documented skill as an experimentalist. Lee told Wu that he and an associate, Chen Ning Yang of the Institute for

Wu's reputation as a superb researcher led other scientists to seek her out when they encountered a roadblock in their research.

Young researchers Chen Ning Yang, *left*, and Tsung-Dao Lee, *right*, sought Wu's assistance in testing a long-standing law of physics.

Advanced Study in Princeton, New Jersey, believed the law of conservation of parity did not hold true for weak nuclear forces. For 30 years, parity was a universally accepted law, considered a cornerstone of atomic decay.

According to the theory, molecules, atoms, and nuclei behave symmetrically. For example, during radioactive decay, atoms act symmetrically by ejecting the same number of particles on the right side of the nucleus as on the left. In other

words, the particles are emitted equally in every direction. This phenomenon is called parity conservation. Consider a person standing in front of a mirror and raising her right hand. The mirror image would show the same person raising her left hand. The physical action of raising the hand is the same in both images, and thus there is so-called parity conservation.

Lee and Yang had conducted several experiments and had studied the scientific literature about parity. They concluded no one had ever proved the universal adherence of atomic particles to this presumed law. They had even written an article about the need for experimentation on parity, noting there was plenty of mathematical proof for the law, but no experimental evidence to either support or refute it. In fact, the law of conservation of parity was so widely accepted that no one had bothered to challenge it under laboratory conditions. "I know of nobody at that time," Yang later recalled, "who believed that it would not be symmetrical."[1]

Wu was immediately interested in exploring Lee's problem. She realized it was a once-in-a-lifetime opportunity to perform a crucial test in her field of expertise, beta decay. Lee was elated when Wu agreed to participate. "Wu had the perception that right-left symmetry was so basic and fundamental that it should be tested," Lee said. "Even if the experiment had showed it was symmetrical, it would still have been a most important experiment."[2] But there was one problem impeding Wu's participation: she had made other important plans for the spring of 1956.

## CHANGE OF PLANS

Wu and Yuan had booked a vacation to celebrate the twentieth anniversary of their arrival in the United States. They planned to sail to Europe aboard the luxury ocean liner *Queen Elizabeth* and attend a physics conference in Geneva, Switzerland. From there, they would conduct a lecture tour in Asia—their first trip to the region since leaving China two decades earlier.

But as a dedicated scientist, Wu wanted to begin work on the parity experiment as soon as possible, fearing another physicist would achieve a momentous finding before she did. She told Yuan to go on the trip alone. Yuan obliged his wife's request and attended the Geneva conference before making stops in England, France, Italy, Egypt, India, and finally Taiwan.

Wu frequently collaborated with other scientists during her career.

Though Wu herself believed the odds of disproving the law of conservation of parity were very slim, she went to work immediately. Her primary objective was to determine the direction in which electrons were ejected from atoms. Nuclei move constantly and rapidly in all directions. As they move, the nuclei generate heat energy. Wu had to eliminate as much of the heat energy as possible so she could determine the direction of the ejected electrons. She needed to make the nuclei of the source material so cold that they barely moved.

Wu chose Cobalt-60, a radioactive isotope of the element cobalt, as the source material, because it could be cooled to extremely low temperatures. Then, a very powerful magnet would be used to force the slow-moving nuclei to line up. The nuclei would continue emitting electrons. Wu hoped the nuclei would remain aligned long enough for her to determine if the electrons were emitted in only one direction, as Lee and Yang had observed in their prior experiments where weak nuclear forces were at play.

Armed with a plan, Wu began to assemble her team of collaborators. The National Bureau of Standards in Washington, DC, had laboratory facilities that could cool materials nearly to absolute zero, the temperature at which atoms transmit no heat energy. The lab was ideally suited to Wu's needs. Next she brought on a team of scientists to help her carry out the experiment. In July 1956, Ernest Ambler, who was highly experienced working with nuclei at low temperatures, and three other colleagues from the bureau joined Wu's team.

Wu's relationship with Ambler, however, got off to a rocky start. In late July, he told her he was taking a two-week vacation and could not start work on the experiment until his return in mid-August. Anxious and unhappy, Wu said nothing, but instead continued her preparations.

Wu collaborated with Ernest Ambler because she needed access to his laboratory, but she was the driving force behind the research on parity.

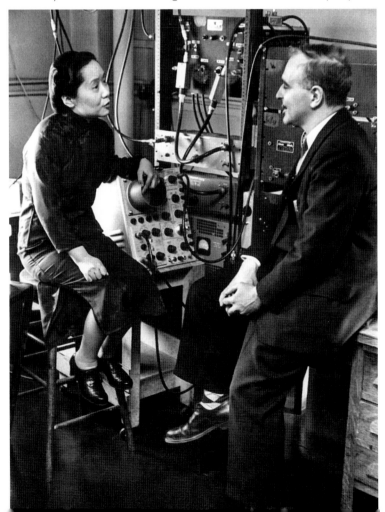

For the next several months, Wu maintained a grueling schedule. She worked night and day, racing back and forth between her teaching job at Columbia and her teammates in Washington, DC, each week.

At times, Wu worried her colleagues in Washington were not working diligently or carefully enough. She was displeased when the team redesigned part of the equipment without her permission while she was in New York. In addition, she was annoyed by the team's habit of playing cards during lunch—time that could have better been spent on the experiment, in her view. Because Wu feared someone else might conduct the experiment first, she pushed herself and her associates to pull out all the stops to complete their work as soon as possible.

By December, Wu's experiments indicated Lee's and Yang's hypothesis had

## Government Standards

In 1901, congressional legislation established the National Bureau of Standards to oversee standardization of weights and measures used in science, industry, and commerce. From 1830 until 1901, this role had been played by the Office of Standard Weights and Measures within the US Department of the Treasury. In the first half of the twentieth century, the National Bureau of Standards also became the nation's main laboratory in the physical sciences. In that role, its research endeavors included tasks such as analyzing the composition of steel and studying the underground corrosion of gas pipelines. In 1988, the agency's name changed to the National Institute of Standards and Technology (NIST), reflecting its mission to support technical innovation and industrial competitiveness. NIST played a key role in investigating the collapse of the World Trade Center following the 9/11 attacks.

been correct. She met with the two scientists at Columbia and told them more electrons were being emitted from one side of the nuclei than the other. She asked them not to make any public announcements, because she wanted to confirm her results. Throughout late December and into January 1957, Wu and her team carefully examined and reexamined their findings.

## Seasoned Experimentalist

Ernest Ambler was Wu's main collaborator on studying parity conservation. Ambler was born in 1923 in Bradford, England. He received his PhD degree from Oxford University. Ambler joined the National Bureau of Standards in 1953 and served as the organization's director from 1978 to 1988. After several phone conversations and correspondence by mail, Ambler met Wu for the first time in September 1956. On her first meeting with the experimentalist, Wu said, "He was exactly as I had imagined him to be from our numerous telephone conversations: soft-spoken, capable, and efficient."[3]

Finally, at 2:00 a.m. on January 9, 1957, the team finished all its tests. Wu and her colleagues were completely satisfied: particles inside the nuclei do not always act symmetrically. The law of conservation of parity had been disproved. The euphoric team celebrated and raised a toast with vintage French wine.

# THE RUSH TO PUBLISH

Wu and her associates now wanted to publish their findings in a scientific journal right away. As originator and designer of the experiment, Wu felt justified writing the paper in private.

She did not discuss its contents with her four collaborators from the National Bureau of Standards. This angered the four scientists, as did Wu's failure to mention them in the body of the paper. When it came time to list the paper's authors, she normally would have appeared last because it was standard practice to list names alphabetically. Wu, however, was unwilling to follow the normal practice, and Ambler courteously allowed Wu to list her name first.

## Edging Out the Competition

Wu's experiment on parity launched her into a race against time as she sought to beat other physicists doing similar research. Before Wu began her work, Yang gave a seminar at MIT in early June 1956, suggesting parity conservation should be tested. Norman Ramsey, a physics professor at Harvard University, was in the audience. Ramsey was intrigued with the idea and immediately began planning an experiment. He contacted Oak Ridge National Laboratory about using its cooling equipment, but he was told another scientist needed it. Ramsey, who would later win the 1989 Nobel Prize in Physics, dropped his plan as a result.

Leon Lederman, a physicist teaching at Columbia University, almost beat Wu in disproving the law of parity. On January 4, 1957, Lee told a group of scientists at Columbia, including Lederman, that Wu's latest results were highly promising. Lederman and a colleague immediately figured out how to design a similar experiment, and by January 7, their positive results were being circulated. Lederman's paper explaining his experiment arrived at the *Physical Review* on January 15, the same day Wu's paper arrived. Both papers were published in the same issue of the journal. The Lederman paper, however, carefully noted how the experiment was started only after hearing about Wu's results.

The paper arrived at the offices of the *Physical Review* science journal on January 15, 1957. It was published in the February 15 issue. The media immediately hailed the major news. On January 16, the *New York Times* ran a front-page headline announcing, "Basic Concept in Physics Is Reported Upset in Tests."[4] National magazines also gave widespread coverage to Wu's experiment. *Time* magazine wrote, "One of [the physicists'] basic laws of nature had been proved not a law at all. From now on their erudite science would never be the same."[5]

Wu, Lee, and Yang became overnight sensations. They appeared on magazines' covers and newspapers' front pages. The three scientists were honored and quoted throughout the world. Wu traveled extensively, speaking at universities and research institutes. "This small modest woman was powerful enough to do what armies can never accomplish," wrote the *New York Post*. "She helped destroy a law of nature."[6] Wu was at the pinnacle of her scientific career, or so she thought.

## The Thrill of Victory

Even the quiet, reserved Wu was elated with the success of her parity experiment. "We were extremely fortunate to have had the opportunity to join in this great venture! These were moments of exaltation and ecstasy," she recalled at a gathering of scientists in 1986. "A glimpse of this wonder can be the reward of a lifetime. Could it be that excitement and ennobling feelings like these have kept us scientists marching forward forever[?]"[7]

# DISAPPOINTMENT AND REDEMPTION

In October 1957, Lee and Yang won the Nobel Prize in Physics. Wu was not included as a recipient of the award. Though the two men had originated the idea that parity did not always apply, Wu had designed and supervised the experiment that confirmed it. She was disappointed not to be named a cowinner of the prize, as were many other physicists who believed she had earned the honor. Even Yang thought Wu deserved to share the award. In 2007, he wrote, "She did not believe the experiment would be so exciting, but believed that if an important principle had not been tested, it should be. No one else wanted to do it!"[8] At the time, Wu never publicly voiced her private feelings about her contribution being undervalued.

Some people believed Wu was not included in the award because she was a woman. Had sexism and discrimination robbed her of the Nobel Prize? Such speculation is impossible to prove, but years later Wu offered her own thoughts on the subject. In a letter to Jack Steinberger, winner of the 1988 Nobel Prize in Physics, Wu wrote, "Although I did not do research just for the prize, it still hurts me that my work was overlooked for certain reasons."[9]

Despite her Nobel Prize snub, Wu had become one of the most esteemed researchers and experimentalists in physics by 1957. That year, she embarked on a long lecture tour of

Europe, speaking in England, Israel, Italy, France, and Switzerland. During the trip, she met old friends from her days at NCU and enjoyed a reunion with her Berkeley companion Ursula Schaefer and Schaefer's husband, Willis Lamb. Lamb had been awarded the Nobel Prize in Physics in 1955 for his discoveries on the structure of the hydrogen atom.

## Innovator and Inventor

Wu excelled not only as an experimentalist but also as a designer and innovator of laboratory instrumentation, including several types of new devices to detect and measure radioactivity. Wu also built a nuclear physics laboratory at Columbia designed to carry out experiments in ultralow temperatures.

Wu soon received many prestigious honors as a result of her accomplishments. In 1958, she was promoted to full professor at Columbia and received an honorary doctor of science degree from her former employer, Princeton University. She was the first female recipient of this degree in Princeton's history. The same year, Wu was elected to the National Academy of Sciences, the most distinguished science organization in the United States. She was only the seventh woman ever elected to the Academy. Wu also won the Research Corporation Award from a private foundation that grants funding for university research. Despite her growing fame, Wu's passion for science never waned—and there would be new conquests to come in the years ahead.

CHAPTER
# SEVEN

# NEW HORIZONS

A hard and dedicated worker such as Wu was not about to rest on her past accomplishments. As a full professor at Columbia University, she kept busy teaching graduate students and developing a strong program in experimental physics. She devised new techniques to study and measure the behavior of nuclei and worked on problems related to X rays.

All the while, Wu looked for new experiments to which she could apply her expertise. Once again, two young men sought her assistance to work on an important new law in nature.

## ANOTHER MAJOR SUCCESS

In 1959, scientists Richard Feynman and Murray Gell-Mann of Caltech called on Wu with a problem, just as Lee and Yang

As her career progressed, Wu widened the scope of her research.

had done three years earlier. The two men had formulated a new law of nature, a hypothesis they called conserved vector current, which helped account for beta decay. Unlike Lee and Yang, however, Feynman and Gell-Mann wanted Wu to conduct experiments that would confirm a theory, not disprove it.

At the time, Wu was busy with her teaching and research commitments at Columbia, and she was unable to help the two men. However, three years later, in 1962, Wu assembled a small team of assistants and began work on the theory hypothesized by Feynman and Gell-Mann. Once again, Wu redesigned a spectrometer for the experiment and carefully prepared and tested her equipment. Other scientists had tried the experiment in Berkeley and Russia, but they had failed to prove the theory. Wu wanted to get it right.

Finally, after many months of planning, experimentation, and gathering data, Wu announced that her results confirmed the theory. She published a paper about the experiment in *Physical Review Letters* in March 1963. Wu's success was yet another critical contribution to understanding beta decay and forces at work on the nuclear level.

## RETURNING HOME

Months before concluding an experiment on conserved vector current in late 1962, Wu, accompanied by her husband, visited

Taiwan. They were attending an important gathering of scientists from her former school, Academia Sinica, which had moved to the small island off the coast of China. It was her first trip to the region since leaving China 26 years earlier. In 1949, the Chinese Communist Party had seized control of mainland China and had established the People's Republic of China. President Chiang Kai-shek had fled China and retreated to Taiwan to set up a separate government.

## Marrying Well

"Behind every great man is a great woman," goes the familiar saying. In the case of Chien-Shiung Wu and Luke Yuan, the opposite was true. Wu benefited greatly from Yuan's strength and support. Yuan encouraged his wife's devotion to science, even if it meant the couple would be apart for long periods of time. Yuan was often their son Vincent's primary caretaker, enabling Wu to spend countless hours in the laboratory conducting research. Wu once commented that a "nice husband," a home near one's work, and reliable childcare were needed for a wife and mother to be a successful scientist.[1] Though Wu and Yuan worked in different areas of physics, in the early 1960s, the couple edited a book together, *Methods of Experimental Physics: Nuclear Physics*. Described by friends as patient, soft-spoken, and considerate, Yuan had the ideal temperament to counteract his mate, who, at stressful times, "could be bossy and opinionated."[2]

Wu gave lectures while in Taiwan, and she was looking forward to a banquet at which she and her beloved teacher-mentor, Hu Shih, were to speak. After the speeches, Hu chatted with the guests as Wu stood nearby. Without warning, the 71-year-old esteemed scholar suddenly turned pale and collapsed to the floor. He had died of a heart attack. Wu was devastated, but she forced herself to complete her lecture tour. Deeply saddened by the tragic loss, Wu and Yuan returned to the United States immediately after she fulfilled her commitments.

The couple returned to Taiwan in July 1965. There Wu saw her uncle, who had funded her trip to the United States and her first year at Berkeley some 29 years earlier. Her uncle was one of Wu's only surviving relatives: her older brother had died in 1958, her father in 1959, and her mother in 1962. Wu had not seen any of them since she left China in 1936. Because the United States had strict restrictions regulating Americans' travel to communist nations, Wu was not able to attend their funerals.

## Women in Physics

In 1965, only 5 percent of the students earning bachelor's degrees in physics were women. That same year, only 2.5 percent of doctorate degrees in physics were awarded to women. Fifty years later, in 2015, one-fifth of both bachelor's and doctorate degrees in physics were earned by women.[3] The current emphasis on STEM (science, technology, engineering, and mathematics) curricula gives girls and young women more exposure to science fields than in the past.

# MORE WORK AND MORE HONORS

In the mid-1960s, Wu conducted an experiment at a bizarre location: in a salt mine approximately 2,000 feet (600 m) below Lake Erie, near Cleveland, Ohio. Wu was investigating double beta decay, a broadening of her

Wu's illustrious career was driven by her love for scientific discovery.

years-long research on beta decay. Her goal was to study the extremely slow radioactivity of radioactive isotopes. Her work space was a small room deep underground. The experiment had to be done in the absence of cosmic rays, the particles that bombard Earth from beyond its atmosphere. The thick salt rock served as a shield, preventing cosmic rays from affecting the experiment. Wu reported her findings in papers published in 1970 and 1975.

At this point in Wu's career, hardly a year passed in which she did not receive an important honor. In 1959, she was given the Achievement Award from the American Association of University Women. This award is presented to women whose achievements span 20 years or more.

In 1963, Wu won the Comstock Prize in Physics, given only once every five years by the National Academy of Sciences for "recent innovative discovery or investigation in electricity, magnetism, or radiant energy, broadly interpreted."[4] Robert Millikan, Yuan's adviser at Caltech, won the award in 1913, and Ernest Lawrence won the award in 1938 for his development of the cyclotron. Wu also won the 1965 Chi-Tsin Achievement Award from a foundation in Taiwan for her work in beta decay and parity. Three years later, she was named an Honorary Fellow of the Royal Society of Edinburgh, presented to individuals "eminently distinguished in any subject."[5]

## "Chinese Madame Curie"

Wu is often called the "Chinese Madame Curie." Marie Curie, a naturalized French citizen, was a physicist who made important discoveries in radioactivity. Born in 1867 in Warsaw, Poland, she and her husband, Pierre, originated the term *radioactivity* to describe elements that emitted strong rays. In 1903, the couple won the Nobel Prize in Physics, and in 1911, Marie won the Nobel Prize in Chemistry for discovering two new elements, polonium and radium. Curie's work led to the use of X rays in medicine, culminating in the field of radiation therapy as a way to treat cancer. Wu's classmates in China and at Berkeley recall Wu being a great admirer of Madame Curie.

As the 1960s drew to a close, Wu had reached the height of her profession. Not only had she earned the respect and admiration of the international scientific community, but she had also become an influential voice encouraging women to enter the sciences. Yet there was still important work for the brilliant physicist to tackle in the years ahead—as well as an unforgettable return to her beloved homeland.

In the 1960s and 1970s, Wu received numerous awards, including an honorary degree from Harvard University, recognizing her contributions to the field of physics.

# EIGHT

# THE LATER YEARS

For many years, Wu was unable to visit mainland China because of travel restrictions to that nation established by the US government. In 1971, however, relations between the two countries began to improve. That year, the US table tennis team went to the People's Republic of China to participate in a tournament, a first step toward easing diplomatic tensions. Soon, several Chinese scientists and scholars visited China, including Wu's parity colleague, Yang, who spent four weeks on the mainland in July 1971. The following year, President Richard Nixon visited China and met with its leader, Chairman Mao Zedong.

Wu's opportunity to visit her homeland had finally arrived. Realizing the chance to return might vanish if United States—

Wu was awarded the much-coveted Tom W. Bonner Prize in Nuclear Physics in 1975.

China relations took a turn for the worse, she and her husband quickly planned their trip home.

# HOME AT LAST

Wu and Yuan visited China in the fall of 1973. Their trip lasted 53 days. In the 37 years since Wu had left China, the nation had experienced a massive social and political transformation called the Cultural Revolution. In 1966, Mao Zedong launched the movement to eliminate what he considered harmful elements in Chinese society. Mao believed many Communist Party leaders were steering the nation to capitalism and had lost their revolutionary spirit. He called on students to help restore the true communist ideals of years past.

Chinese youth responded by forming militant groups that attacked political leaders, scholars, scientists, and older Chinese citizens. The violent movement spread to parts of the Chinese Army. Important cultural sites and historic artifacts were destroyed. Approximately 1.5 million

## Traveling Abroad

During the 1970s and 1980s, Wu and Yuan traveled extensively, with Taiwan a frequent destination. The couple served as advisers on the nation's synchrotron radiation program. A synchrotron is a football field–sized machine used for research that accelerates electrons to nearly the speed of light. Wu and Yuan met with the president of Taiwan and convinced him Taiwan needed a synchrotron. The president agreed, and the project was completed within ten years. In 1988, Wu returned to Liuhe to attend a commemoration of her father's one-hundredth birthday. She donated money to establish the Wu Zong-Yi Memorial Foundation, which would grant scholarships and fund education for teachers at Ming De School.

Posters and other propaganda materials disseminated by the Chinese Communist Party aimed to create loyalty to communist ideals among young people.

people were killed during the Cultural Revolution, and millions more around the country were persecuted, imprisoned, and tortured.[1] The ten-year movement was eventually brought to a stop through the actions of Chinese premier Zhou Enlai, who by 1970 had assumed greater control of the government. Years earlier, Zhou had played a role as a student leader in the May Fourth Movement, a political movement that favored Western ideals over traditional Chinese values. He also arranged the historic meeting between Mao Zedong and President Nixon in 1972.

During their 1973 visit, Wu and Yuan toured many cities and towns, including Wu's birthplace, Liuhe. They met many old friends, and in private, the friends spoke of the horrors they had experienced during the Cultural Revolution. Wu learned her younger brother and the uncle she visited during her 1965 trip to Taiwan had been tortured to death during the revolution. She further learned the graves of her parents had been destroyed during the violence.

## All in the Family

Like his parents, Vincent Yuan displayed a keen passion for science. His mother insisted he attend the highly regarded Bronx High School of Science, a short train ride from the family's apartment in Manhattan. When Vincent graduated, Yang, Wu's associate from her parity-experiment days, advised the young man to study biology, suggesting he attend a school outside New York City. Instead, Vincent decided to attend Columbia University and major in physics. He received his undergraduate and graduate degrees from Columbia and performed postdoctoral work at the University of Illinois. Vincent then took a position as a research scientist at the Los Alamos National Laboratory in New Mexico, where he worked for many years.

Wu and Yuan also met with Premier Zhou. The Chinese leader apologized for the suffering Wu's family had endured and the destruction of her parents' graves. Wu was impressed with Zhou's sincerity and polite manner. Nevertheless, her trip to China was a painful episode and a bitter reminder of the hardships her fellow Chinese suffered in the years during her absence. The couple returned to China several more times in subsequent years.

## MEDICINE MATTERS

Wu had spent many years studying beta decay. In the mid-1970s, she turned her expert hand to a new field: medical science. In 1974 and 1975, Wu conducted experiments to investigate the structure of hemoglobin, a protein in red blood cells. Red blood cells play a critical role in humans, carrying oxygen throughout the body. These cells also remove carbon dioxide from the body, carrying it to the lungs to be exhaled as a waste product. Hemoglobin contains molecules that have iron atoms. In the lungs, the iron atoms bond with oxygen atoms. The red blood cells then move throughout the body, releasing the oxygen.

Wu decided to study hemoglobin and sickle cell anemia, a disease caused by deformed red blood cells that is most common in people of African origin. Hoping to better understand the disease, Wu investigated why some hemoglobins attracted oxygen easily but some did not. Her work helped shed

# SCIENCE
# SPOTLIGHT

## SICKLE CELL ANEMIA

Red blood cells, with the help of hemoglobin, supply life-giving oxygen to the human body. Healthy red blood cells are round with an indented center. This shape allows them to move easily through the bloodstream, carrying oxygen to all parts of the body. The red blood cells of people with sickle cell anemia are shaped like half-moons, making it difficult for the cells to move smoothly through blood vessels. The sickle cells get stuck in the vessels and clog the flow of blood. In addition, sickle cells live only 10 to 20 days, compared with red blood cells' normal life-span of 90 to 120 days. This rapid die-off means the body has a hard time manufacturing enough red blood cells and hemoglobin to keep up with the deficit, resulting in anemia. People with sickle cell anemia often feel tired or weak from lack of oxygen, and pain can result from blockage of a blood vessel. In extreme cases, the disease can cause infection and even death. Sickle cell disease is a genetic condition that usually becomes evident in infancy if it is present.

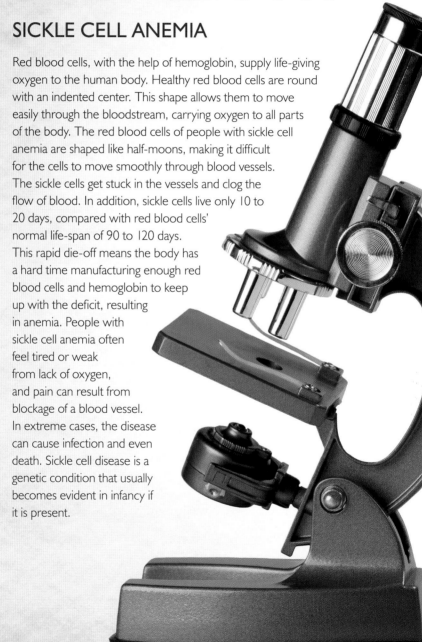

light on the disease, encouraging other scientists to conduct further research. "This case illustrated that even a seemingly remote, fundamental nuclear research technique can benefit society," she said.[2]

## PRAISE FROM PEERS

As the years passed, Wu's impressive body of work continued to garner the acclaim of her peers. In 1973, Wu was appointed the first Michael I. Pupin Professor of Physics at Columbia University. Columbia established the special award to honor Mihajlo Pupin, a noted Serbian-born American physicist who studied and taught at Columbia in the 1880s and 1890s. In 1974, Wu was named Scientist of the Year by *Industrial Research* magazine. The following year, the American Physical Society awarded Wu the Tom W. Bonner Prize in Nuclear Physics.

The honors continued to roll in. In 1975, Wu won the National Medal of Science, the nation's highest science award, presented by President Gerald Ford. Three years later, she received the Wolf Prize in Physics from the Wolf Foundation in Israel, widely regarded as the most esteemed award in physics apart from the Nobel Prize. In 1986, the Statue of Liberty–Ellis Island Foundation gave Wu the Ellis Island Medal of Honor to celebrate the one-hundredth anniversary of the Statue of Liberty. Wu was one of 80 recipients chosen from among 15,000 notables nominated for the honor.[3]

In 1985, the Institute of China presented Wu with the Second Blue Cloud Award for her contributions to cultural exchange between China and the United States. Both Wu and Yuan received the Achievement Award from the Institute of China in 1994, celebrating their work in physics.

Wu received her most unusual honor in 1990, when the Purple Mountain Observatory of the Chinese Academy of Sciences in Nanjing named Asteroid #2752, discovered in 1965, the *2752 Wu Chien-Shiung*. Wu was the first living scientist to be given the honor.

## Barrier Breaker

In 1975, Wu was elected president of the American Physical Society (APS). The APS is one of the world's foremost science organizations, advancing physics knowledge through journals, meetings, and international activities.

Wu's election was a monumental event. She was the first woman ever to hold the honored position, and the first Chinese American, male or female, to serve as APS president. Though still working full-time at Columbia University, Wu tackled her position with spirit and enthusiasm. Believing the science community should communicate with the general public, she gave frequent interviews to newspaper, magazine, and television reporters. She wrote articles in APS journals discussing problems facing the sciences and suggested solutions physicists should pursue.

In October 1975, Wu wrote a letter to President Gerald Ford asking the president to ensure the government would provide steady and sufficient funding for scientific research. Ford agreed and set up a special department within the White House to provide the president and senior staff with scientific advice on important matters. That department still functions today as the Office of Science and Technology Policy.

Wu joined an elite group of scientists when she was selected to receive the National Medal of Science.

## THE FINAL YEARS

In 1980, at age 68, Wu retired and was named professor emeritus at Columbia, allowing her to retain her old office and library privileges. During the rest of the 1980s, she often spent time in the library and visited with colleagues. By the 1990s, her health began to decline as she suffered from high blood pressure and severe headaches. Wu began to spend less time at Columbia and more time at her apartment in the Bronx.

Wu had a heart attack in 1995 but survived with the aid of a pacemaker. On February 16, 1997, at age 84, she died after suffering a stroke.

## WU'S LEGACY

Though a brilliant, meticulous, and painstakingly precise researcher and experimenter, Wu was often overlooked for promotions and honors during the early years of her career. Ultimately, her strong character and indisputable abilities made her one of the world's preeminent physicists as she tested theories, designed experiments, and resolved baffling problems of science. "Ask Miss Wu" was the advice given by one scientist after another when a colleague needed to solve a problem.

Wu broke long-standing barriers, both as a woman and a Chinese American. Through her undeniable competence as a scientist and her legendary work ethic, she triumphed over the discrimination directed at her because of her gender and ethnicity. Wu's singular focus on science helped set standards of excellence in research and experimentation, which she passed on to a generation of budding physicists. Many of her scientific findings were revolutionary—whether supporting new theories or disproving ones that had long been accepted as true. Wu was an outspoken supporter of human rights and women in science, and she strongly believed scientific advancement could one day cure society's ills.

In 1992, the Chinese government opened the Chien-Shiung Wu Laboratory in the center of Nanjing, the city where Wu had attended NCU many decades earlier. The facility is one of the most important research laboratories in China and serves as the principal lab for the Ministry of Education. Here, and in universities around the world, young students continue to learn about Wu's remarkable successes.

Wu's memory also lives on at Nanjing University (formerly NCU) in the school's Chien-Shiung Wu Memorial Museum. The modern, three-story building features photos of Wu working in her laboratory, meeting with dignitaries, and enjoying the company of friends. Shelves and walls are lined with many of the honors and awards presented to Wu. The museum also has a library displaying books and manuscripts used by Wu during her years of study and research. A model of the equipment used by Wu on the parity experiments is a popular attraction. Wu's husband donated many of his wife's possessions after her death to help create the museum.

In 2001, Leon Lidofsky, professor of applied physics

## Speaking Her Mind

Throughout her adult life, Wu urged women to choose science as a career, and she eagerly addressed the issue on many occasions. In a panel discussion on Women in Physics in 1971, Wu said, "Men have always dominated the fields of science and technology. . . . They have pushed us to the brink of environmental disaster. Air, lakes, rivers, and oceans have all been polluted. . . . The world would be a happier and safer place to live if we had more women in science."[4]

and nuclear engineering at Columbia, wrote of his colleague, "[Wu] will always be remembered, by those who were her students, not only for her contributions to her field, but also as a caring mentor who expressed interest in those with whom she worked. All of us can wish that, when presented with such opportunities, we can respond as well."[5]

Wu made a lasting impact in the field of physics and on the many students she taught and mentored.

# TIMELINE

## 1912
On May 31, Wu Chien-Shiung (later known as Chien-Shiung Wu) is born in Liuhe, China.

## 1921
Wu graduates from her father's school and begins studying at Soochow Girls High School.

## 1929
Wu graduates from Soochow and is admitted to National Central University (NCU).

## 1934
Wu earns a diploma from NCU.

## 1936
In August, Wu travels to the United States intending to enroll at the University of Michigan. She enrolls at the University of California, Berkeley instead.

## 1940
Wu receives a PhD degree in physics from Berkeley and works there as a research assistant. The Manhattan Project begins.

## 1942
In May, Wu marries physicist Luke Yuan; the couple moves east, where she takes a teaching position at Smith College.

## 1943
Wu becomes the first female professor at Princeton University.

## 1944
In March, Wu joins the top-secret Manhattan Project and becomes a research scientist at Columbia University.

## 1947
Wu and Yuan's son, Vincent Yuan, is born.

## 1949
Wu proves Enrico Fermi's theory of beta decay.

## 1957
Wu disproves the law of the conservation of parity.

## 1958
Wu becomes a full professor at Columbia and is elected to the National Academy of Sciences.

## 1963
Wu publishes proof of the theory of conserved vector current and receives the Comstock Prize in Physics from the National Academy of Sciences.

## 1975
President Gerald Ford presents Wu with the National Medal of Science. She becomes the first female president of the American Physical Society.

## 1978
Wu wins the esteemed Wolf Prize in Physics in Israel.

## 1980
Wu retires after 36 years as a researcher at Columbia.

## 1990
The Chinese Academy of Sciences names an asteroid after Wu: *2752 Wu Chien-Shiung.*

## 1997
On February 16, Wu dies of a stroke at the age of 84.

# ESSENTIAL
# FACTS

## DATE OF BIRTH
May 31, 1912

## PLACE OF BIRTH
Liuhe, China

## DATE OF DEATH
February 16, 1997

## PARENTS
Wu Zong-Yi and Fan Fu-Hua

## EDUCATION
Elementary school at Ming De School, Liuhe, China
Soochow Girls High School, Suzhou, China
National Central University, Nanjing, China
University of California, Berkeley, PhD in physics

## MARRIAGE
Luke Yuan (May 30, 1942)

## CHILDREN
Vincent Yuan (born 1947)

## CAREER HIGHLIGHTS
- In 1944, Wu was enlisted as a senior scientist for the Manhattan Project, a top-secret effort sponsored by the US government to develop an atomic bomb. Wu worked on nuclear fission in a laboratory at Columbia University.

- Using a spectrometer she created, Wu proved Enrico Fermi's theory of beta decay in 1949.

- In 1957, Wu's research disproved the law of the conservation of parity, a long-held principle in physics. Colleagues Yang and Lee were awarded the Nobel Prize in Physics for their part in the work, but Wu was excluded from the award.

- Wu's experiments confirmed the theory of conserved vector current in 1962.

- Broadening the scope of her research to medicine, Wu investigated causes of sickle cell anemia in 1974 and 1975.

- In 1975, Wu was elected first female president of the American Physical Society and was awarded the National Medal of Science by President Gerald Ford.

## SOCIETAL CONTRIBUTIONS

- Wu's research contributed to the development of the atomic bomb, the use of which hastened an end to World War II. Scientists' understanding of beta decay and parity, two cornerstones of physics, was substantially enhanced by Wu's work.

- Wu's legendary work ethic and high standards in the laboratory influenced a generation of physicists as to the proper way to conduct scientific experiments.

## CONFLICTS

- At the age of 24, Wu left China to study in the United States. She would never see her parents or brothers again.

- Wu was unable to visit her homeland because of US travel restrictions to communist countries in the 1950s and 1960s.

- Working in a traditionally male field, Wu faced prejudice and discrimination as a female physicist. She also faced discrimination as a Chinese American at a time when Asians in the United States were viewed with suspicion.

## QUOTE

"I sincerely doubt that any open-minded person really believes in the faulty notion that women have no intellectual capacity for science and technology." —Chien-Shiung Wu

# GLOSSARY

### anglicize
To adapt to English usage.

### collaborator
A person who works with others on a project.

### exempted
Freed from doing something others are required to do.

### experimentalist
A person conducting scientific experiments.

### fusion
A process releasing vast amounts of energy through the union of nuclei.

### hemoglobin
The protein in red blood cells that carries oxygen throughout the body.

### isotope
One of two or more forms of the same element.

## matriarch
A woman who rules or dominates a family or an activity.

## sickle cell anemia
A disease caused by deformed red blood cells, resulting in poor oxygen transport within the body.

## spectrometer
A device that analyzes wavelengths of light to determine what elements are present.

## stipend
A fixed, regular payment for a service performed.

## subatomic
Of or relating to a process that occurs within an atom.

## symposium
A meeting or conference.

## visa
An official authorization permitting entry into and travel within a country.

## X ray
A form of electromagnetic radiation.

# ADDITIONAL RESOURCES

## SELECTED BIBLIOGRAPHY

Chiang, Tsai-Chien. *Madame Wu Chien-Shiung: The First Lady of Physics Research.* Singapore: World Scientific, 2014. Print.

Howes, Ruth H., and Caroline L. Herzenberg. *Their Day in the Sun: The Women of the Manhattan Project.* Philadelphia: Temple, 1999. Print.

McGrayne, Sharon Bertsch. *Nobel Prize Women in Science: Their Lives, Struggles, and Momentous Discoveries.* Washington, DC: Joseph Henry, 1998. Print.

Reynolds, Moira Dawson. *American Women Scientists: 23 Inspiring Biographies, 1900–2000.* Jefferson, NC: McFarland, 1999. Print.

## FURTHER READINGS

Vander Hook, Sue. *Manhattan Project.* Minneapolis, MN: ABDO, 2011. Print.

Young-Brown, Fiona. *Nuclear Fusion and Fission.* New York: Cavendish, 2017. Print.

## WEBSITES

To learn more about Women in Science, visit **abdobooklinks.com**. These links are routinely monitored and updated to provide the most current information available.

# FOR MORE INFORMATION

For more information on this subject, contact or visit the following organizations:

## Field Museum Women in Science
1400 South Lake Shore Drive
Chicago, IL 60605
312-922-9410
https://www.fieldmuseum.org/about/employee-groups/women-science
Part of the historic Field Museum, the Women in Science group promotes the work of women and minority scientists in their academic and professional careers.

## L. R. Ingersoll Physics Museum
Chamberlin Hall, University of Wisconsin–Madison
1150 University Avenue
Madison, WI 53706
608-262-4526
https://www.physics.wisc.edu/ingersollmuseum
The museum's exhibits give visitors a hands-on experience of concepts ranging from mechanics to modern physics in an easy-to-understand presentation.

## National Museum of Nuclear Science & History
601 Eubank Boulevard SE
Albuquerque, NM 87123
505-245-2137
http://www.nuclearmuseum.org
The museum offers artifacts and exhibits that tell the story of the Atomic Age, from early research of nuclear development through the ways nuclear technology is used today.

# SOURCE NOTES

## CHAPTER 1. MADAME PHYSICIST

1. Rita Levi-Montalcini. "Reflections on Scientific Adventure." In *Women Scientists: The Road to Liberation*, edited by Derek Richter. New York: MacMillan, 1982. Print. 111.

2. Chiang Tsai-Chien. *Madame Wu Chien-Shiung: The First Lady of Physics Research*. Singapore: World Scientific, 2014. Print. ix.

3. Rita Levi-Montalcini. "Reflections on Scientific Adventure." In *Women Scientists: The Road to Liberation*, edited by Derek Richter. New York: MacMillan, 1982. Print. 111.

4. "Queen of Physics." *Newsweek* May 20, 1963: 20. Print.

5. T. A. Frail. "The Injustice of Japanese-American Internment Camps Resonates Strongly to This Day." *Smithsonian*. Smithsonian, Jan. 2017. Web. 6 Mar. 2017.

## CHAPTER 2. A STAR IS BORN

1. Sharon Bertsch McGrayne. *Nobel Prize Women in Science: Their Lives, Struggles, and Momentous Discoveries*. Washington, DC: Joseph Henry, 1998. Print. 259.

2. Ibid. 260.

3. Ibid.

## CHAPTER 3. COMING TO THE UNITED STATES

1. Sharon Bertsch McGrayne. *Nobel Prize Women in Science: Their Lives, Struggles, and Momentous Discoveries*. Washington, DC: Joseph Henry, 1998. Print. 262.

2. Chiang Tsai-Chien. *Madame Wu Chien-Shiung: The First Lady of Physics Research*. Singapore: World Scientific, 2014. Print. 49.

# CHAPTER 4. GOING EAST

1. "Julius Robert Oppenheimer." *NuclearFiles.org.* Nuclear Age Peace Foundation, 2017. Web. 10 Nov. 2016.

2. Sharon Bertsch McGrayne. *Nobel Prize Women in Science: Their Lives, Struggles, and Momentous Discoveries.* Washington, DC: Joseph Henry, 1998. Print. 265.

3. "US Inflation Calculator." *US Inflation Calculator.* Coinnews Media Group, 2015. Web. 10 Nov. 2016.

4. Chiang Tsai-Chien. *Madame Wu Chien-Shiung: The First Lady of Physics Research.* Singapore: World Scientific, 2014. Print. 74.

5. William Dicke. "Chien-Shiung Wu, 84, Dies; Top Experimental Physicist." *New York Times.* New York Times, 18 Feb. 1997. Web. 26 Jan. 2017.

6. "Bombings of Hiroshima and Nagasaki—1945." *Atomic Heritage Foundation.* Atomic Heritage Foundation, 5 June 2014. Web. 6 Mar. 2017.

7. "Burma Road." *Encyclopedia Britannica.* Encyclopedia Britannica, 2017. Web. 3 Jan. 2017.

8. Chiang Tsai-Chien. *Madame Wu Chien-Shiung: The First Lady of Physics Research.* Singapore: World Scientific, 2014. Print. 77.

9. Ibid. 58.

## CHAPTER 5. BETA DECAY

1. Sharon Bertsch McGrayne. *Nobel Prize Women in Science: Their Lives, Struggles, and Momentous Discoveries*. Washington, DC: Joseph Henry, 1998. Print. 270.

2. Ibid.

3. Chien-Shiung Wu. "The Discovery of Nonconservation of Parity in Beta Decay." In *Thirty Years Since Parity Nonconservation: A Symposium for T. D. Lee*, ed. Robert Novick. Boston, MA: Birkhäuser, 1988. Print. 28.

4. Sharon Bertsch McGrayne. *Nobel Prize Women in Science: Their Lives, Struggles, and Momentous Discoveries*. Washington, DC: Joseph Henry, 1998. Print. 269.

5. Ibid.

6. Ibid. 271.

7. N. Benczer-Koller. "Personal Memories of Chien-Shiung Wu." *Physics and Society* 26.3 (1997). *American Physical Society*. Web. 6 Mar. 2017.

## CHAPTER 6. PARITY BREAKTHROUGH

1. Sharon Bertsch McGrayne. *Nobel Prize Women in Science: Their Lives, Struggles, and Momentous Discoveries*. Washington, DC: Joseph Henry, 1998. Print. 273.

2. Chiang Tsai-Chien. *Madame Wu Chien-Shiung: The First Lady of Physics Research*. Singapore: World Scientific, 2014. Print. 126.

3. Chien-Shiung Wu. "The Discovery of Nonconservation of Parity in Beta Decay." In *Thirty Years Since Parity Nonconservation: A Symposium for T. D. Lee*, ed. Robert Novick. Boston, MA: Birkhäuser, 1988. Print. 30–31.

4. "Basic Concept in Physics Is Reported Upset in Tests." *New York Times*. New York Times, 16 Jan. 1957. Web. 6 Mar. 2017.

5. "Science: Death of a Law." *Time*. Time, 28 Jan. 1957. Web. 6 Mar. 2017.

6. *New York Post*. January 22, 1959. In *The American Women's Rights Movement*, by Paul D. Buchanan. Wellesley, MA: Branden, 2009. *Google Book Search*. Web. 6 Mar. 2017.

7. Chien-Shiung Wu. "The Discovery of Nonconservation of Parity in Beta Decay." In *Thirty Years Since Parity Nonconservation: A Symposium for T. D. Lee*, ed. Robert Novick. Boston, MA: Birkhäuser, 1988. Print. 35.

8. Christine Sutton. "Rooted in Symmetry: Yang Reflects on a Life of Physics." *CERN Courier*. Institute of Physics, 30 Jan. 2007. Web. 6 Mar. 2017.

9. Chiang Tsai-Chien. *Madame Wu Chien-Shiung: The First Lady of Physics Research*. Singapore: World Scientific, 2014. Print. 148–149.

## CHAPTER 7. NEW HORIZONS

1. Sharon Bertsch McGrayne. *Nobel Prize Women in Science: Their Lives, Struggles, and Momentous Discoveries.* Washington, DC: Joseph Henry, 1998. Print. 267.

2. Chiang Tsai-Chien. *Madame Wu Chien-Shiung: The First Lady of Physics Research.* Singapore: World Scientific, 2014. Print. 242.

3. "Percentage of Women in Physics." *APS Physics.* American Physical Society, 2017. Web. 3 Jan. 2017.

4. "Academy Honors 17 for Major Contributions to Science." *National Academies of Sciences.* The National Academies of Sciences, Engineering, and Medicine, 15 Jan. 1999. Web. 3 Jan. 2017.

5. "Laws of the Society." *Royal Society of Edinburgh.* Royal Society of Edinburgh, Oct. 2014. Web. 3 Jan. 2017.

## CHAPTER 8. THE LATER YEARS

1. "Cultural Revolution." *History.* A+E Television, n.d. Web. 6 Mar. 2017.

2. Chiang Tsai-Chien. *Madame Wu Chien-Shiung: The First Lady of Physics Research.* Singapore: World Scientific, 2014. Print. 249.

3. "80 Named as Recipients of Ellis Island Awards." *New York Times.* New York Times, 16 Oct. 1986. Web. 6 Mar. 2017.

4. Chiang Tsai-Chien. *Madame Wu Chien-Shiung: The First Lady of Physics Research.* Singapore: World Scientific, 2014. Print. 189.

5. "Chien-Shiung Wu." *Proceedings of the American Philosophical Society* 145.1 (March 2001). *American Philosophical Society.* Web. 16 Nov. 2016.

# INDEX

# ABOUT THE
# AUTHOR

Nel Yomtov is an award-winning author of nonfiction books and graphic novels for young readers. His writing passions include history, geography, military, nature, sports, biographies, and careers. Yomtov has also written, edited, and colored hundreds of Marvel comic books. Yomtov has served as editorial director of a children's nonfiction book publisher and as executive editor of Hammond World Atlas book division. Yomtov lives in the New York City area with his wife.